This Bo...
Heartfelt Thanks
To:

Heartfelt Thanks®

for Serving in Children's Ministry

Group®

Loveland, Colorado

www.group.com

Heartfelt Thanks for Serving in Children's Ministry

Visit our Web site: **www.group.com**

Credits

Contributing Authors: Enelle G. Eder, Ellen Javernick, Keith D. Johnson, Trish Kline, Katie Martinez, Julie Meiklejohn, Larry Shallenberger, Kelli B. Trujillo, Roxanne Wieman, Vicki L. O. Witte
Editor: Sue Lerdal
Creative Development Editor: Mikal Keefer
Chief Creative Officer: Joani Schultz
Copy Editor: Alison Imbriaco
Art Director: Jean Bruns
Book Designer/Illustrator: Liz Malwitz Design
Children's Art: Jordan Johnson, Harmony Kline, Keri Lehr
Cover Art Director: Bambi Eitel
Cover Designer/Illustrator: Marianne Richmond Studio, Inc.
Production Manager: Dodie Tipton

ISBN 0-7644-2765-2
10 9 8 7 6 5 4 3 2 1   14 13 12 11 10 09 08 07 06 05
Printed in Singapore.

Table of Contents

Introduction

It may have been something as simple as a smile or a pat on the shoulder at just the right moment. Or perhaps it was something a little more involved—a specially prepared meal that taught you about people in other lands… a song or Scripture you never forgot…the gift of your very own Bible. Whatever that small but meaningful gesture was, a children's ministry worker from your past left a lasting impression on you during your childhood. In fact, he or she may have inspired you to return the favor someday. And now there are children today whose lives will never be the same…because of your efforts.

Won't it be worth it to one day hear the words, "Well done, good and faithful servant"? Thank you for serving in children's ministry— you *do* make a difference.

Mr. Slaughter was the most enthusiastic and positive adult I knew in my church's fourth-grade midweek program. I always counted on his goofy yet sincere grin, clapping hands, and tireless encouragement: "Great job, Keith!" "You can do it!" "Fantastic!"

Whether I was competing on a sports field or in the classroom, he communicated with both verbal and nonverbal expressions that I was important and that my efforts counted highly.

I don't remember if I placed first or last, but I still remember the power of those encouraging words.

♥ Read John 14:16. The Holy Spirit is sometimes called Comforter or Counselor—one who comes alongside to help. How are comfort and encouragement similar?

♥ Practice expressing encouragement with your eyes and mouth in front of a mirror, first smiling and then not smiling. How do tone and expression make a difference?

My Journal Response

To encourage means to "inspire with courage"—to give a can-do feeling. Encouragement is a gift we give to others.

How can you use your voice to encourage others? Who needs your encouragement today?

mforter
Counselor

Lord,
Please use my voice, eyes, and tone
to encourage somebody the way I was encouraged.
In Jesus' name, amen.

Waiting and Watching

During my elementary years, my mom sang in the choir, and that meant church could last for hours. To kill time, I would ditch Sunday school and run around exploring our extensive church building and grounds.

At those times, Mr. Larry, the Sunday school superintendent, seemed to be everywhere! I always got caught and would be given a choice: go back to my mom or back to class. (I always chose class!)

But Mr. Larry never scolded me. Like the father in the story of the prodigal son, he patiently waited and watched for me and then set me back on the path I needed to be on.

♥ Read Matthew 26:40. What keeps you watching and praying for your students?

Look through one end of an empty paper towel tube, and focus on one person in a group. How does the tube help you lock out distractions? How could you likewise focus on a student who needs extra attention?

My Journal Response

"Seek and you will find…"
points you to the path for pursuing
God's will in life.

How can I help those students who
have wandered far from God to
find the path back to him?

Lord,
*Show me those who have
wandered away from you,
and help me to pursue them
the way you always pursue me!
In Jesus' name, amen.*

Peace That Transcends

David, our youth minister, had the practice of arriving early before each youth-group Bible study and praying for each of us by name, asking God to wrap us in the peace, love, and acceptance we needed.

The gathering would then typically begin with a song calling forth the "sweet Spirit…of the Lord." At first, the stresses and pain of life might still be evident on our young faces, but within moments, our inner turmoil would melt into peace, "the peace of God, which transcends all understanding."

It was the sweet peace of the Holy Spirit, invited there by David's prayers.

♥ Read Philippians 4:7. How can you help your students experience peace that "transcends all understanding"?

♥ Help your youth define peace by defining what peace is not: fear, worry, or stress. Make a list of Scriptures, such as Matthew 6:25-33, that encourage them to seek Jesus' peace.

"And the peace of God, which transcends all understanding, will guard your hearts and your minds in Christ Jesus."

Dear God,
Thank you for your peace.
Please help me to help others discover your peace too. Amen.

Breaking the Mold

Tom and Jenna did not fit the mold of "typical" Sunday school teachers. Jenna was a colorful young adult who expressed her personality through bold fashions and interesting jewelry. Tom, her assistant, was a college freshman who availed himself endlessly to our fourth-grade class.

My parents hesitated to leave me in the class because these teachers seemed so unconventional, but Tom and Jenna were truly qualified for their ministry. That year I learned more Scripture than any year before—or since!

♥   Read 1 Timothy 4:12. When have you been looked "down" on? How did that make you feel?

♥   Make a list of your strengths and weaknesses, taking into consideration your talents, age, background, and training. How can your weaknesses, as well as strengths, help you to minister effectively to children? Reflect upon your list whenever you doubt your qualifications.

My Journal Response

I can't do everything, but God equips me to do things that no one else can.

When do I lack confidence? Why? What do I feel equipped to do right now?

Dear God,
I desire the daily confidence to
not worry about breaking the mold.
Thank you for using me just as I am to
teach and encourage children. Amen.

The Pine Cone in the Parking Lot

The doctor's words rang in my ears: "Positive biopsy…immediate surgery…mastectomy." Crying, I almost didn't see the pine cone in the parking lot.

Suddenly, I was a teenager again, sitting near a campfire at church camp. Our counselor was holding up a pine cone and explaining that it contained seeds we couldn't see—only during the heat of a forest fire would the seeds pop out. But from the ashes, the seeds would flourish, sprout, and mature into sturdy new trees.

God, she said, had likewise given us inner strength to grow again after devastating life events.

The pine cone at my feet brought back her words— with God's help, I, too, could grow again.

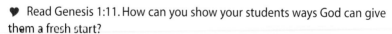

♥   Read Genesis 1:11. How can you show your students ways God can give them a fresh start?

♥   Plant a bulb, such as an amaryllis or a paperwhite narcissus, that your students can watch sprout and flower. Discuss how the bulb can be saved and replanted to flower again, and compare the bulb's new life to the chances for rebirth that God gives to your students.

My Journal Response

The more things stay the same,
the more likely they are to change.

How can I prepare myself to accept
changes with serenity?

Dear God,
As I'll bloom where I am planted,
encourage me to find new soil regularly. Amen.

Going the Extra Mile

Every Sunday morning Sister Helen's rusty station wagon would pull into the church parking lot, full of "unchurched" children from her neighborhood. She loved the Lord, and she wanted to bring the children to church to hear the Word of God.

Sometimes that meant going into their homes and dressing them herself. Other times, she would promise them a bottle of soda, a bag of chips, or a trip to Dairy Queen after church. Sister Helen was not wealthy, but she used whatever means it took to convince the children to come to church.

Sister Helen inspired me at that early age to one day do likewise and go the extra mile to reach out to children for God. And I have!

💜 Read 2 Timothy 4:2. How much are you willing to inconvenience yourself for someone else?

💜 Give a hug, a flower, or a note of encouragement to someone who "goes the extra mile." Let that person know how appreciated he or she is.

Dear God,
*Please give me wisdom to see
the needy children out there
and bring them to you. Amen.*

Above and Beyond

We were new to the church, and I was reluctant to get involved. The children's ministry director, Karin, knew this and went out of her way to invite me to play a special role in the Christmas musical. My family was thrilled for me!

Karin arranged to pick me up after school, and together we'd run through lines and practice songs at the church office.

Then came the big performance. I felt special, included, no longer an outsider in a big church. Karin had gone above and beyond for me, and I would never be the same again.

♥ Read Ephesians 6:6-7. When did you last extend a special invitation to a lonely child? What happened?

♥ Who are the children and families you know and influence? Which ones could use a special invitation? a ride? a card? Plan this week to invite them to a church activity, and let someone know your plans—then follow through!

My Journal Response

Everyone longs to belong.

Which children in my class need
my focus this week?
How can I help them feel they belong?

Dear God,
*Please inspire me with ideas and simple gestures that could
mean the world to children, and give me the self-discipline
to follow through with them! Amen.*

Taking God's Love to the World

My fourth-grade teacher once did a series on the foreign missionaries our church supported. We learned about the countries where they served, the people they ministered to, and the languages, foods, and spiritual beliefs of those people.

She even made a peanut soup from Indonesia that we ate with our fingers as we sat on the floor!

From then on, we began to personally connect to our missionaries in ways we never had before. We better understood who we were praying for, where they were, what struggles they were facing. And later, three classmates went on mission trips themselves.

♥ Read Matthew 28:19-20. What are some ways you can help your students be missionaries to others?

♥ Pray for your church's missionaries, and contact them to ask for specific prayer requests. Then have your students pray for them and send cards and letters.

My Journal Response

Missionaries share God's love in unfamiliar and uncomfortable places, often with those who won't accept it.

How can I keep showing God's love when someone who doesn't know him resists it?

Dear God,
Help me to pray for missionaries, here and abroad, and to equip my students to take your love to the world too. In Jesus' name, amen.

The Gift That Lasts

Mrs. Hautamacki, my children's church teacher when I was in third grade, had a passion to communicate the gospel, and she did so each and every Sunday.

One morning when she extended an invitation for salvation, my sister Jeanine raised her hand, signaling that she had asked Jesus into her heart.

Not to be outdone, I raised my hand too! Mrs. Hautamacki knew that I was simply following my sister's lead. She nevertheless repeated the invitation, and I asked Christ to be my forever friend.

In her willingness to share "the gift that lasts," this dear woman made a difference in my life—for eternity!

♥   Read Ephesians 2:8-9. What happened the last time you shared the gospel message with a child?

♥   This week, write out your testimony—the eyewitness account of what God has done for you—in one concise paragraph. Then share it with someone.

Dear God,
Please help me share my story
and draw children to you
so that they'll have
their own stories to tell.
In Jesus' name, amen.

Matthew

MARK

LUKE

John

Special Talents

Stuart was a professional guitar player who assisted in our church's youth group. He soon discovered which of us students were interested in music and invited us to play our instruments as he led the singing.

Eventually, Stuart asked me to play piano in a Christian band he had started, and in college, I began leading worship on my own for various groups and churches.

Stuart was the first person to invite me to use my musical talents to help others. Today, I coach worship leaders all over the country and help churches renew and revitalize their worship services.

♥   Read Proverbs 22:6. What training could you provide others, and who could benefit from that training?

♥   Make a list of people who have mentored you—teachers, parents, friends, co-workers. Now make a list of talents, skills, hobbies, and special interests you have. Which children or young adults do you know who could benefit from your mentoring?

My Journal Response

Mentoring includes showing someone
the places you've been and sharing the
things you enjoy.

Whose teaching was most effective
in my life and why?

Dear God,
*Thank you for providing me with
special training and the opportunities
to pass on what I have learned. Amen.*

At the start of each preteen Sunday school class, our teacher would deal with some of the more, um, *energetic* boys' hyperactivity by getting everyone's wiggles out right away. She'd yell out a word like *grasshopper* or *stars*, and we'd race to various concordances around the room, flip through them, find a verse, run back to our Bibles, and yell it out. What a blast!

I didn't realize it then, but our teacher was prompting us to use a Bible study tool. Not many people expect fourth graders to use concordances! But our teacher *did*, and her fun "game" equipped me for a lifetime of in-depth personal study of Scripture.

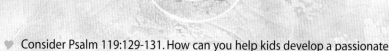

♥ Consider Psalm 119:129-131. How can you help kids develop a passionate desire for God's Word?

♥ Pique a preteen's interest in pursuing personal Bible study with a journal, devotional book, age-appropriate study Bible, or subscription to a devotional magazine.

My Journal Response

It's been around for thousands of years, yet God's Word never gets old.

How can I use Bible study tools or other resources to deepen my relationship with God?

Dear God,
Help me plant seeds in kids' lives that will grow into a flourishing passion for studying your Word. Amen.

Pass It On

For years I struggled with receiving kindness from others, not out of ungratefulness, but rather from guilt because I couldn't always repay the kindness.

When friends stepped in to help while our youngest daughter was in the hospital, I fretted, "I'll never be able to repay you."

"Don't worry," one friend said. "I'm just passing on help I've received."

She told me about hearing the story of the good Samaritan in Sunday school. The man on the road to Jericho couldn't repay the Samaritan, her teacher had explained, so he passed on that kindness to another.

My friend was remembering the lesson she'd learned long ago and passing it on to me. Now I remember the lesson and pass it on too.

♥ Read Luke 10:30-35. How have people passed along the good Samaritan's kindness to you?
♥ Come to class with a Band-Aid on your forehead. When your students ask about it, tell them the story of the good Samaritan.

"Then he put the man
on his own donkey,
took him to an inn and
took care of him."

Dear Lord,
*Help me watch for opportunities to help others so I may be part of
the unending chain of caregivers. Amen.*

Bringing It Home

I was seven years old when my parents divorced and my mother found herself needing child care for three school-age children. She was too tired to take us to church on weekends, so our baby sitter, a faithful Sunday school teacher, would teach us Sunday school lessons right in her own back yard.

Mary Jane became a source of spiritual support for my entire family. My siblings and I would go home in the evenings and tell our mother what we had learned about Jesus. Eventually, we began attending church and Sunday school.

Today, my siblings and I disciple others much as Mary Jane discipled us.

♥ Read Deuteronomy 6:4-9. How can you share God's love and character with others?
♥ Keep a written record of the Scriptures and themes of lessons you prepare. As you document your journey, you'll interact with the message on a deeper level, grow in Bible knowledge and confidence, and influence children in your neighborhood—and your own home!

My Journal Response

Tell the story in the marketplace,
and watch the church grow.

Who outside church—
child or adult—
can I share these lessons with?

Dear God,
Help us transform your world
and bring home the message
of your church. Amen.

Words Live Forever

Although they were not youth ministers, Ray and Anita often lovingly opened their home to our youth group.

One evening, we sang a song based on Isaiah 40:30-31. I still recall the joyful message: "Even youths grow tired and weary…but those who hope in the Lord will renew their strength…"

Anita's eyes caught mine, and her beautiful voice sang out as the other voices faded away. I began to really *listen* to the words—they seemed to come alive in my spirit.

In times of difficulty, I remember Anita's singing, and those cherished words come alive again: We are promised strength as we hope in the Lord.

They will soar on wings like eagles

♥ Read Colossians 3:16-17. How does your life reveal that Jesus Christ dwells in you?

♥ Think of someone whose life demonstrates the Word of God living in him or her. What character traits does that person have? Make a list, and refer to it during daily prayer.

My Journal Response

The Word of God is Jesus Christ, alive and living inside me.

How can I use my words to encourage someone else today?

Dear God,
*Please make your words
come alive in me,
so that my words may
guide and uplift others—
maybe even years later.
Amen.*

Encouragement for the Road

Talk about humiliating.

We ninth graders—still in junior high—had been invited on a trip to an amusement park with the senior high youth group.

The park was located a good distance away. In fact it was in the next time zone. My friend and I somehow misunderstood what time we were supposed to meet back at the vans—and we showed up an hour late. We "kids" felt terrible about making everyone else wait because of our mix-up.

I almost cried, but the new youth leader assured me that he knew it had been an innocent mistake. His encouragement boosted my confidence—and rather than slink off in embarrassment, I remained a youth group member throughout high school.

♥ Read 1 Thessalonians 2:11-12; 5:11. How do you encourage your students?

♥ Arrange to attend an event—a game, a recital, a play—that a student you know is participating in. Take him or her out for a treat afterward and encourage the student further.

"For you know
that we dealt with each of you
as a father deals with his own children,
encouraging, comforting
and urging you
to live lives worthy of God,
who calls you into his kingdom
and glory."

Dear God,
*Thank you for your cloud of
witnesses who cheer me on.
Help me to encourage
others along the road as
I am encouraged. Amen.*

The Broken Window

Explaining death is never easy.

As I planned how to comfort my students after the loss of their classmate, I recalled a story a Sunday school teacher once told me. A church custodian broke a beautiful stained-glass window. Devastated, he stored the pieces because he couldn't bear to throw them away. Years later, an artist remade the window, and the new one was even more beautiful than the old one. In fact, it glowed as if light lived inside it.

Death is like the broken window, my teacher explained, and God is the Master Craftsman who gives us a new, more beautiful life.

It was my turn to pass on the story.

♥ Read 2 Corinthians 1:3-4. How can you pass along comfort you once received to someone grieving today?

♥ Encourage children to share memories and photos of family members, friends, or pets who have died. Arrange the photos on a large heart, and label it "Alive in Our Hearts."

My Journal Response

Don't wait until tomorrow to share love today.

If my loved ones died tomorrow, would I regret something left unsaid?

Dear God,
You're a God who comforts those who are broken, hurting, and hopeless. You understand us. Help us understand children who are in pain. Amen.

Before My Earliest Memories

My faith was shaped even before my earliest memories.

I didn't realize it until I took my newborn son to the church nursery for the first time and handed him over—with great apprehension.

After a few weeks, my nervousness disappeared. I saw how my son was held, rocked, tenderly cared for…and *prayed* for. The nursery workers were making an eternal investment as they became "spiritual parents" to my son each Sunday morning.

I don't personally recall any details—faces, voices, names—of the people who cared for me in infancy. I don't remember anything they said or did. Yet I do know this: They significantly shaped my first understanding of God's love as they made me feel content, secure, and treasured.

♥   Read about God's comforting love in Isaiah 43:1-4a. How can you show kids that they're precious in God's eyes?

♥   Minister beyond words this week. Pile on the smiles! Shower kids with meaningful eye contact, affirming expressions, and appropriate physical affection.

36

My Journal Response

Jesus loves the little children—
all the children of the world.

What does the tender care
parents provide for infants
reveal about God's love for me?

"I have summoned you by name;
you are mine."

Dear God,
*Let everything in my demeanor
communicate your effusive
and amazing love. Amen.*

A Cure for Acne

I can't remember what point my fifth-grade Sunday school teacher, Mr. Wagner, was trying to make that day. It may have been something about how we could prevent acne by washing our faces thoroughly with soap and water—as if good hygiene were an important biblical truth to be imparted.

I *do* remember he cared enough to speak on topics that mattered to us, a room full of pimply preteens standing on the edge of change. Mr. Wagner had entered our world.

Now, whenever I stand in front of a room full of kids, I'm reminded to enter their world.

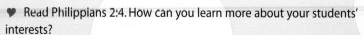

♥ Read Philippians 2:4. How can you learn more about your students' interests?
♥ List your needs and then list your students' needs. Use the lists to remind yourself to place their needs before your own.

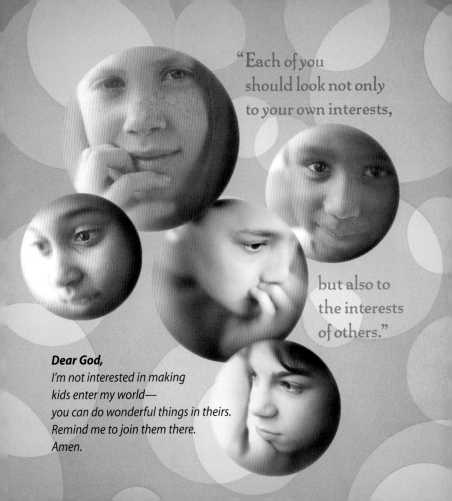

"Each of you should look not only to your own interests, but also to the interests of others."

Dear God,
*I'm not interested in making
kids enter my world—
you can do wonderful things in theirs.
Remind me to join them there.
Amen.*

Praise With Gusto

Frank filled many roles in my life, from Sunday school teacher in junior high to confirmation mentor to great personal friend. But his greatest influence on me was as a member of the adult choir.

In church, my family always sat close to the front, where we had a good view of the choir. As soon as the first note of any song sounded, Frank's face would break into a huge grin, and he would begin to worship. He praised God with gusto!

Every time I watched Frank sing, I wanted to praise God too.

 come before him with joyful songs

♥ Consider Psalm 100. How can you praise Jesus so visibly and audibly that your students are encouraged to join you?

♥ Teach your students praise songs, share favorite psalms and other worshipful Scriptures, or set up a "Praise Board" where students can post their own expressions of praise to God.

My Journal Response

"Gratitude makes sense of our past, brings peace for today, and creates a vision for tomorrow" (Melody Beattie).

If I kept a "praise journal" and each day listed God's gifts to me that day, how much would I have to praise God for at the end of a week?

Dear Lord,
Help me to express my joy outwardly.
In Jesus' name, amen.

A Family Affair

I was cast—"casted" might be a more accurate term—into children's ministry at an early age.

One evening my parents brought the whole family along to paint a room that would be used for children's church. While they worked, my brother and I, one room over, built a tower of chairs atop a table. I climbed on top. And like the walls of Jericho, my tower and I came tumbling down!

My parents rushed me to the ER, and my elbow was reset. I wore a cast for weeks. I barely remember the pain from that incident, but I do remember the fact that my parents had grabbed a paintbrush and *gotten involved* to help make children's church a great place to be—for my sake.

♥ Read Deuteronomy 4:9-10. How can you encourage your students' parents to get involved in their children's development?

♥ Review your class roster. Do any kids need "surrogate spiritual parents"? Pray and ask God to assign them an adult mentor.

My Journal Response

God is our Father. But he often shows us his parental love through his caring followers.

Who are my "spiritual parents," and how have they influenced me?

Dear God,
Help me to inspire parents to be spiritual
champions of their children. Amen.

A Shepherd's Crown

During college, I spent summers leading Kids Krusades.

One evening near the end of service, a stranger entered and sat down. I was telling a story about a little boy who received a crown in heaven for praying with his doctor and nurse to follow Jesus Christ. As I encouraged the children who desired the same to come forward for prayer, many responded.

After the service, the stranger approached me and asked, "Will you get a crown in heaven for all the little kids who came up to the front tonight?"

I never saw the young man again, but I still remember his question, and I ask myself, "Are my motives for serving in children's ministry worthy of a crown from the Chief Shepherd?"

because you are willing

♥ Read 1 Peter 5:2-4. What example do you set for those you lead?
♥ Cut sheep shapes from white card stock. Write, "*Ewe* are a blessing to our flock," on the cards, and give them to the children's ministry leaders in your church.

"And when the Chief Shepherd appears, you will receive the crown of glory that will never fade away."

Dear God,
Help me to lead your sheep as a willing servant. Amen.

A Catchy Tune

My parents were probably annoyed that I sang "Matthew, Mark, Luke, and John…" to the tune of "Yankee Doodle" over and over, day in and day out. But it *wasn't my fault!*

My Sunday school teacher was to blame. She taught our class the books of the New Testament in canonical order using that catchy tune. We'd sing it each week. The result? The song—and the names of the New Testament books—became forever embedded in my brain.

Decades later, I still sometimes burst out in song during Bible study or quietly whisper the song while looking up a certain verse. My teacher made learning fun by using a creative pneumonic device—singing—and it stuck!

♥ Read Psalm 63:6-8. How can you make Bible learning "stick" so that kids remember God day and night?

♥ Use a unique object to help students "see" a scriptural truth, or set a Bible verse to music to help students retain it.

My Journal Response

Let God's Word, like seed falling on fertile ground,
take root deep in your heart.

Dear God,
*Thanks for creating our brains with
long-term memory! Help me deliver
your truth so that it really "sticks." Amen.*

The Most Excellent Way

Every year our elementary Sunday school classes would put together care packages filled with fun, practical things for the church's college students. We'd include gum, Ramen noodles, gift certificates, coffee, and toothpaste. We had fun and got excited about college—and the day we would get our own care packages!

Whether shopping for goodies, finding boxes, looking up addresses, or keeping us fed with pizza, our teachers did everything in the most excellent way. It wasn't just a job to them. At some time, they had taught most of the college students these boxes were for…and still cared deeply for them.

That's how I knew that my teachers would always care for me, too.

♥   Read 1 Corinthians 13:1-3. How are you showing a ministry that is based upon love?

♥   Think about some of the kids you've taught over the years. Pray for them in their current lives and roles and, if possible, write letters or send cards.

My Journal Response

Love—not guilt or obligation—
should be the motivation for all our actions.

How does doing something out of obligation
differ from doing something out of love?

Dear God,
*Help me to serve and love my students
as your Son served and loved us.
In Jesus' name, amen.*

Apple Pie Order

One evening, frustration toward a co-worker—and a request for apple pie—brought to mind a summer Bible school lesson from my childhood.

Mrs. Bertodi had brought apples from her tree. They were covered with a foggy film, and she polished them as she talked.

"People are like apples. You can't always see the good inside them." She placed an apple on its side and sliced through it. Then she held up one half and pointed out the seeded star right in the center. "God wants us to look for the good in others," she told us.

Now, as I prepared the pie, I cut an apple in half. There was the star! I vowed to look for the good in my co-worker.

♥ Read Matthew 13:46. What beautiful things, like pearls within oysters, lie hidden inside your students?

♥ Make this weekend's chores time a time of prayer. As you dust, vacuum, or mow the lawn, ask God to open your eyes to the beauty inside your family members.

"When he found one of great value,

he went away and

sold everything he had

and bought it."

Heavenly Father,
Help me to look beyond outward appearances into the hearts of others. Amen.

The Treasure of the Word

One squirrelly morning in fifth-grade Sunday school class, I had "forgotten" my Bible. My teacher, Mr. West, found out and loaned me his own tattered one.

As we worked through the lesson, I noticed that nearly every verse I looked up—and most of the verses next to them—had markings of some sort. Highlights. Mr. West really took this book seriously.

When I returned the Bible, Mr. West paused. "Do you need a Bible?" he asked.

"Yes." (I think I lied.)

"the word of God is living and active"

"Here, use mine."

I learned that day that a loving, caring teacher used his Bible…a lot!

♥ Review Hebrews 4:12. What are some ways you reveal the value of God's Word to your students?
♥ Close your eyes and try to identify each key on your key ring. Which one fits your front door? your car? How does being able to select the right key compare to being able to rightly use your Bible?

My Journal Response

"I have hidden your word in my heart." We often assume that this phrase refers to memorizing God's Word, but in this case, *hidden* means "treasured" or "valued highly."

How can I teach children to treasure the Word in their lives?

Dear God,
Thanks for the truth
preserved for us in your Word! Amen.

Unconditional Love

My earliest memories of Sunday school include my teacher, Miss Huisjen. I think I fell in love with Jesus partly because of her kindness in showing me Jesus' love. (Years later, I volunteered to teach a Sunday school kindergarten class so that I, too, could share Jesus' love with children.)

One Christmas, Miss Huisjen gave me a small ring made of copper with a pink enamel coating. On the band was a picture of a dove carrying an olive branch. The gift was probably inexpensive, but to a child it was priceless.

I looked for the ring today. It appears that the ring and I have become separated. But I am confident that nothing can ever separate me from the love of God in Jesus Christ.

♥ Read Romans 8:38-39. How do you show your students God's unconditional love?

♥ Spend some time this week just hanging out with students. Don't try to teach them anything; just enjoy being with them—and let it show.

My Journal Response

As important as good curriculum and well-planned lessons are, most children will likely remember how you made them feel.

How do the kids in my class feel God's unconditional love through me?

Dear God,
Thank you for loving me no matter what.
In Jesus' name, amen.

Sweet Voices

As I slid into the pew, I was still reeling from the dreaded pink slip I'd received. It wasn't fair!

Organ music interrupted my thoughts. The children's choir filed in. Their sweet voices transported me back to the time I sang in children's choir. Our director always reminded us to think about the words we sang.

Suddenly, one of the songs he'd taught us popped into my mind: "Jesus… has a plan for your life, and you know he'll always be there."

In the months that followed, I often hummed that tune. Changes did come, but God had a plan for my life. He would always be there.

plans to give you hope and a future

💜 Read Jeremiah 29.11. Consider opportunities God has provided. What plan does he have for the way you'll influence the children you work with?
💜 Think about how the words in your favorite hymns can give you encouragement and hope. Sing some of your students' favorite songs with them, or play some modern gospel music as background music.

"For I know the plans I have for you."

Dear God,
Help me be open to the plans you have for me, even in dark times. Amen.

I Can Do It!

Mrs. Ussery was young, pretty—and new. She didn't do things the way our other Sunday school teachers did them.

She *asked* who wanted to read—she didn't assign verses. She let us create crafts out of strings, glitter, (edible!) mint paste, and feathers. And she didn't hold up samples of finished crafts that I could never quite replicate.

Mrs. Ussery let us be creative. By allowing us to make choices, she taught us the power of initiative. Because of her, I have never stopped learning!

♥ Review 1 Thessalonians 2:7. How can treating children with gentleness help them develop independence and a love for learning?

♥ On one table, set out blank sheets of paper, crayons, glitter, glue, and yarn; on another, set out just crayons and preprinted coloring sheets. Observe which activities the children choose. What do their choices say about their learning preferences?

My Journal Response

Winston Churchill said, "Personally I'm always ready to learn, although I do not always like being taught."

How can I guide my students better by *not* teaching them to do something?

Lord,
Help me not to do for my students what you have created them to do for themselves—
learn and grow. In Jesus' name, I pray. Amen!

A Wise Suggestion

I was young when my family moved. Lacking enthusiasm for an unfamiliar place of worship, we attended church sporadically.

I noticed that several children in my third-grade Sunday school class had new, red Bibles—gifts for Promotion Sunday. I asked if I could have one. The teacher, reading my hesitation to commit, wisely suggested that I earn a Bible by attending class three weeks in a row.

I influenced my family to attend consistently, received the Bible, and committed to what eventually became my middle and high school youth group.

"he should ask God"

♥ Read James 1:5. What wisdom from God do you need for challenges you're facing?

♥ With Bible in hand, review your class list. Ask God for wisdom to notice your students' special needs and personalities. As you reflect on each child, jot down notes, and refer to them as you pray for the children in coming weeks and months.

My Journal Response

The classroom is a colorful place. Each child adds the distinct shades of his or her special needs and special contributions.

Who needs my extra attention this week?
How can I craft an experience for that child?

Dear God,
Please give me wisdom to lead and teach my students according to their unique gifts and needs. Amen.

Seeing the Future Me

"I see such a precious spirit within you for loving God...I'll always know that somewhere you're singing and sharing Jesus."

Miss Pat wrote these words in the back of the hymnal she gave me when I "graduated" from children's choir.

In her letter, Miss Pat spoke a *vision* into my life. She instilled in me a sense of future—a future of strong, unshakable faith in Christ. She ministered to me as a kid, all the while praying and hoping for the adult I would someday become.

Miss Pat saw the *future* me...and helped me see it too.

♥   Read what Paul wrote to the young man he mentored in 2 Timothy 1:1-8. How might Paul's encouragement have influenced who Timothy became as he grew older?

♥   Speak *vision* into the life of a child. Write a letter (perhaps as part of a keepsake) describing the child's positive traits and the strong faith you hope he or she will have as an adult.

"For this reason I remind you

A SPIRIT OF POWER,

to fan into flame

OF LOVE

the gift of God."

AND OF SELF-DISCIPLINE

Dear God,
Make me a "Paul" in a young "Timothy's" life. Amen.

Thank You